Speak Easy Poets

by the Speak Easy Poets
of Topeka, Kansas

Published by Top City Records, 2024

While every precaution has been taken in the preparation of this book, the publisher assumes no responsibility for errors or omissions, or for damages resulting from the use of the information contained herein.

SPEAK EASY POETS

First edition. August 7, 2024.

This Machine Builds Community

www.topcityrecords.com

Table of Contents

This anthology is dedicated
to the mighty
Annette Hope Billings,
"Maya of the Midwest",
co-founder of Speak Easy Poets,
and spiritual mother
to so many of Topeka's poets,
writers, and artists.
She, along with Sue Edgerton-Johnston,
has created Speak Easy Poets
in her own image
warm, safe, and welcoming,
creative and bright,
honest and brave."

Annette Hope Billings

Annette Hope Billings is an award-winning poet and actress living the blues in a red state. Her most recent poetry collection is *Just Shy of Stars*. Billings' work has appeared in numerous anthologies and journals. To learn more about her and watch her perform: anetfullofhope.net

Speak Easy

In the hunt for her,
duties, stamped urgent, in hand,
don't search in a fray of tasks which allegedly can't wait.
She'll not be located in a litany of line items
or be manacled in a milieu of must-be-dones.
She will have abandoned the queue for unanswered questions
and vacated the vicinity of adult responsibilities.

Instead, search a water's edge
where, with spiral notebook and number 2 pencil nearby,
she'll likely be found in poet's repose
appreciating cat's paw ripples across a lake.

Only when she turns her face back toward the road
should you easily speak her name.

Posted: No Trespassing

My body is my birthright,
my property,
my ground.
No one holds a lien on its caverns or fields,
there is no acreage to commandeer here,
no hills at the mercy of legislation.
My body is not subject to imminent domain
or governmental seizure,
and no right-of-way courses through it.
My surrounding borders are not negotiable,
each one, solely mine to declare.
I say what grows on it, in it,
I am free to sow orderly crops in uniform rows
or let the whole of it grow indelibly wild with Big
bluestem and Switchgrass with not a single blade of
opinion.

My body is my birthright,
my property,
my ground.
GET OFF MY LAND!

Diane Silver

Diane Silver is a Pushcart Prize-nominated poet and essayist who publishes the *Poetry & Life* newsletter and podcast. (DianeSilver.Substack.com). Her work has appeared in *Ms, The Progressive, MockingHeart Review*, and many other publications. Her books include the *Daily Shot of Hope* meditation series.

To the Woman I Loved Too Soon

Now that it's legal for us to marry
I wonder if you and I have become glass.
We're here—but maybe not—
transparent unless held up to the light
turned so the glow from some lamp glances off
to show us all those years ago
in bed falling asleep holding hands,
in our kitchen leaning together as you stir a pot,
in our living room dancing in bare feet,
sitting on the floor outside our toddler's room
because it's 2 in the morning, he won't stop crying,
all the books say let him cry until he falls asleep.
We last a whole five minutes before barging in.
I pick him up, you curl around us both.
Together we sing him to sleep.

If some stranger should come close enough
to brush a hand against the thin sheet of our lives
he might catch on the moment
we arrived home to see every
ceramic pot you ever made (except one)
on the floor in pieces, probably knocked off the table
by our cat who inspected them after you left them there
because we were late for the appointment
where the doctor said your cancer came back.

You picked up that last pot, held it so long I thought:
it's ok. she's handling this, then you threw it down
to smash, shards skittering across tile.
You leaned on the table, inhaled.
I was thankful to be there to hold tight
as you shook in my arms on that day
twenty-two years before we could wed
three months before you were dead.

Everything ends. Every love that doesn't end
in argument ends in death. Yet I worry. What
will happen to we who weren't allowed to marry?

Generations of us have been swept from time.
Will you and I become another glass shattered?
Will all our pieces get left behind?

~

An earlier version of this poem was published in The Coop.

Me, Defined

Double chin. Big belly. Ample bosom. Short.
A man's cropped hair. Lesbian. Dyke. Use the old
slang, say *bulldagger*. If I were allowed to hobnob
with debutantes, I'd be in the back of the ballroom.
They'd be bending willows in their white ball gowns,
crinoline-stiffened skirts, their arms bare. Even in
my best jeans, crisp white shirt (collar up), black blazer,
I'd be the boulder. Too big to be fashionable. Too weird
to be heard. I'm the one the kids at school laughed at.
The one thing you never wanted to be if you were a girl.
The one whose kind has never blessed a magazine cover.
The one who blushes even though I feel about myself
the way roots must feel about their oak, the way
the sea must feel about its tallest wave,
the way I hope you feel someday.

~

An earlier version of this poem was published in The
Lavender Review.

Prophecy

In the mud of our lives a day will come
when every mother screaming at her daughter,
every father punching his son, everyone pointing
a gun, every crook rifling through somebody's
bank account, every lawmaker voting queers
out of existence, every CEO pocketing a bonus
for separating people from their jobs, every
righteous person taking hostages, every
general bombing cities, every man loving
a woman's fear, every person sneering
at someone with skin darker
than their own, every bully
on every playground
in the world, all of us
all at once will stop.

Mouths will shut. Fists will unclench,
Guns will be put down. Fingers will be
pulled away from launch buttons.
Hostages will be released unharmed.
Anyone standing in front of anyone
they've badgered into crying
or trembling or looking even
a tiny bit ashen will step back.

Some of us will search for Kleenex.
A few old-fashioned souls will take
handkerchiefs out of pockets or purses.
Wet eyes will have to be wiped before
we've collected ourselves enough
to turn to each other and say
I am so sorry.

Days will pass, months, then years.
All the needle-tipped words, all our shame
will dissolve into puddles that will evaporate.
Someday someone will win a Nobel Prize
for discovering that what we assumed
were the ropes of our captivity were actually
the threads of our cocoon. By that time,
the sky will be filled with fluttering.
Our wings will carry us everywhere.

~

An earlier version of this poem was published in The Coop.

Fred Appelhanz

Living on 30 acres gives me many opportunities to experience the beauty, wonder and vastness of Nature. Also, having traveled to almost all of the states West of the Mississippi River has exposed me to a variety of people and lifestyles. I look forward to my next adventure as I grow older.

Rusty

Rusty's eyes danced
with wide-eyed excitement.
He had been empowered by
the ultimate commitment.

His mind was freed
of all questions or doubts.
The power of life or death
was his to bring about.

He was always reminded
of courageous heroes long gone.
Given a simple mantra
to be forever strong.

Rusty never was a killer,
growing up timid and jovial.
The military gave him manhood;
a lifestyle aggressive and maniacal.

His training complete
as orders were given.
Among salutes and parades
to the battlefield he was driven.

Rusty would join
the millions before;
as a pawn of the power elite
achieving the goals of war.

Morning Love

Whisper sweet sounds,
laced with the emotion
of a thousand kisses.
For my body craves
the esoteric ecstasy
of your touch.

Let the world contract
into a singular moment,
as we drift into
a fog of enchantment.
Safely in infinity's embrace,
all questions disappear.

Time is suspended
within two heartbeats,
beating as one.
Two breaths quiver,
melting into each other,
breathing as one.

Love silently simmers,
as arms and legs enfold
the essence of contentment.
Only intimacy can ignite
passion so genuine,
love so real.

Honey

When a sunset reveals its magnificence,
in wondrous hues and delights,
taking my breath away;
I will whisper your name.

In the stillness of a moonlit night,
enfolding all senses with its serenity,
giving my soul reassurance;
I will whisper your name.

And as life evolves in heartfelt experiences,
capturing moments of incredible clarity,
bringing a smile to my heart;
I will whisper your name.

Or the sound of rain, sight of snowflakes,
reminders of intimate conversations,
causing me to tremble;
I will whisper your name.

The cuddling of lover's fingertips,
while listening with only their eyes,
witnessing a universe of just two;
I will whisper your name.

Pleasures of consoling assurance,
dwell in your laughter and smile,
when magic stirs the air;
I will whisper your name.

In a baby's eyes, hints of amazing secrets,
or in an embrace of true tenderness,
and in a glancing touch of love;
I will whisper...

When the night is completely silent,
the only sound, one beating heart,
my soul searching for solace;
I will...

Anamarie Davis-Wilkins

Anamarie Davis-Wilkins is a published writer, poet, and birth doula who loves to travel as well as read and perform open mike. Her work has been featured and published in numerous anthologies and online magazines. Some of her works were featured in and by the Poet Laureate of Kansas, Discourse Literary Journal, and The Write Bridge Journal 2024. She has two collections of poetry, *Reminiscence* and most recently, *To See My Own World*. She is currently putting the finishing touches on her second novel.

A Time!

Do you remember that day?
I mean are you hip to when
people stood shoulder to shoulder,
everyone was accepted
and ignored color.

It was power to the people!
Right on! Right on!
Jimi Hendrix, psychedelic, supersonic funk,
with hippie flowers,
black power
The revolution will be televised.

Yet, there was peace, love,
shots fired, beatdowns,
fists up, gobs of spit,
cracked skulls, fires blazing,
burning tears that make you choke,
riots in the streets
hope gone up in smoke.

Marvin Gaye's "What's Going On" blaring,
Stop the war! No to Vietnam shouts, Maryjane, and
psychotropics
all that didn't stop the brotherly love,
but it was not the love that Dr. King spoke about.

That was years of time
and time this time,
it's guns, crack and crank to get lit,
zombies frozen in place,
blank eyes stares and senseless crimes
just to buy the next hit.

What happened melting pot?
Yes, it was the "Me Decade"
it was decided,
that it was time to escape and look inward
to find oneself.
It was a place in time when we were here nor there
but everywhere.

Were we disillusioned with the strikes,
the wishes, and the want.
Are we living that continuing circle of time,
and it's still all about "me".

For today it takes
tragedy and catastrophe,
before we stand
shoulder to shoulder,
everyone is accepted,
color ignored
and then, it becomes "We".

My Identity

It's as plain as Jane,
not clear as crystal,
cloudy before the rain.

It's of multicolored layered rainbow
of different nationalities.
Primary colored paints blended together
to make the color black.

But not that definition of black.
I am as brown as melted milk chocolate
with a hint of red chili powder.

A black woman, mom, grandmother,
writer, poet, and birth doula.

Older and active,
chubby but confident,
graying and wise,
black and proud.

All these hold the role,
meaning, and expectations of me.
My Identity!
Now watch me evolve.

All in the Walk

As I walk, it is with
confidence, pride, and control.

As I walk, it is with
my whole being of creativity
and sensibility.

As I walk, it is only
women like myself,
who knows the struggles
in the footsteps I leave behind.

As I walk, it is with
the attitude and toughness,
that I have adorned because
of past inequalities.

As I walk, it is with
wit and courage,
that will take me
a step closer to victory.

Renee Washington-Akers

I'm not much of a writer, but occasionally something comes from my musings. The two poems I submitted are ripped from my heart from the extremes of emotion, from joy and exhilaration in the first to sadness, grief and loss in the second. And they are about the same person, same relationship.

I can not thank Annette Billings enough for caring so deeply about literally everything, but most especially about each of us and our words. And for providing the safest place to share the most vulnerable of writings with people who will just love and care for the writer. I am lucky to know her and lucky to be a part of Speak Easy Poets.

Devotional aka The Beginning aka Alpha

I lick my lips as I lower myself to my preferred altar.

Smooth, soft skin with the smell of coconuts followed quickly by the musk of your arousal, mine leaping to respond as I force myself to slow down.

Nose and lips caress the innermost flesh of your thighs and I feel you shudder with desire. Barely brushing that sweet spot of skin where your thigh meets hip and hip meets pelvis and I lay my prayers there in wait for the devotional to come.

My hands, thus far kept still at my sides, slide slowly, lazily and yet with purpose up your outer thighs, pulling them gently apart, laying bare the inner sacristy of where I will lay my prayers.

One last glance at your face before descending, my lips full, mouth watering at the decadence that awaits. The sheer magnitude of that first taste of the ambrosia that meets my hot tongue and I am lost and drowning, yet unafraid.

My tongue dancing across that delightful bundle of nerve endings that are screaming out for me to sing their song and release the chorus of your opus. Swirling softly and murmuring my devotional onto you and into you.

Coaxing every last bit of pleasure with no set end game other than your complete release.

I am pulled from the reverie by the sound of your voice chanting over and over, the prayer you've chosen for me and I know it's time. My devotional has changed in pitch and tempo to match your ever increasing chanting. Drawing out the final climax of our magnificent composition, and you throw your head back and the howl of release has at last come.

I whisper into your inner sanctum, Amen, and at last my devotional is complete.

Ghost Band aka The End aka Omega

I wonder if there is a blemish on your ring finger, as there is on mine.

A mark to prove we happened. I wonder when it will fade.

Does it itch? Mine does. In moments of great sorrow, grieving what we were, what we could have been.

What we should have been.

Why does everything feel so wrong now? When everyone is thrilled to see me "back to myself" but I feel so hollow and broken and unworthy of good.

Is there a mark on your finger too? Does it feel wrong to you too? Do you think we may find each other again one day?

I don't know that I want the answers to those questions. Either way will hurt. What's done is done, right?

There is beauty in the ashes that were us, beautiful things growing anew and blooming. Things that have nothing to do with you, but because of the lack of you, they grow. But that emptiness is still a grey sky with thunderheads, threatening to drown me, while the sun shines and love grows elsewhere.

How do I let go? Haven't I let go? Most days, I feel as if I have. But then. Something happens.

I hear a song. I see a photo. I get a text.

Or I see my ring finger.

Does yours still bear witness to us? Does it remind you that we were each other's Alpha and Omega once? That you were the match to my gasoline?

I wonder when it will fade from view. I imagine I'll always feel the gravity of what we once were or maybe what I thought we would be in that ghost band on my finger.

Duane L. Herrmann

Duane L Herrmann has carried baby kittens in his mouth, pet snakes, and has conversations with owls, but is careful not to anger them! He writes poems, history, memoir and more and enjoys moonlight most of all.

After Auschwitz

To write, after Auschwitz, is obscene
but to not write at all
would be far, far worse:
we MUST write, but differently.
We must write so that
<u>NEVER</u>, EVER AGAIN
will killing become
a way of life, a profession,
a bureaucratic purpose
or occupation.
We must NOT be silent
nor forget
Armenians, Jews, Hutus,
Tootsies and all the rest
murdered for who they were
not what they did.
"The diversity of the human family
should cause love and harmony."

Aftermath

Weeks afterward
the party was held
as scheduled:
darkened room decorated
and refreshments –
no school
for this last hour.

<u>BANG!!</u>

Silence.
The students froze.
"Lights,"
calmly the principal called.
"It was a balloon,
no one else is here,"
she explained
to children's wide-eyed fears.
No one is shooting us…
this time.

The Wind's Own

Wind:
    roaring, howling –
        wild, screaming
    shrieking into every crack –
        shrilly, demonically.

Wind:
        incessantly calling –
            pleading, pulling, prying;
    never letting up –
        continually, mercilessly.

Alone –
    on the hill, the woman stood;
                surrounded by the wind
        crying though the grasses –
                        pushing clouds along.

She tried to see a house,
            or person,
        but no,
    she was alone,
            no other human evidence.

Alone –
    no one for miles –
        Just grass and hills and wind.
            her mate away to pay the claim
        she joined the wind.
        shrieking, howling, crying...
                she was sister to the wind.
        They ran the hills together:
                companions.

The wind had claimed its own.

Up and down, she ran and rolled,
        stumbled,
    unaware –
  and ran again.

Crying, shrieking...
    she was found
            running with the wind.

No human here,
    she fought loving arms around her:
            a creature of the wind.

She has her peace now,

The wind does not trouble her
    on the Hill of Silence –
        caressed
            by the breeze.

Johnnie Xel

I have been writing and performing poetry for many years. I've read in LA, Denver, Tucson, Phoenix, Tempe, Topeka, and Kansas City MO.

I currently reside in Topeka Kansas, with my cat, and the human that I love and adore. I continue writing because the world keeps turning.

I write about personal struggles, being transgender, and political concerns. I have self-published and sold several collections of poetry.

Speak Easy Poets was where I first read poetry in Kansas and they welcomed me as one of their own.

You can reach me at johnniexel@gmail.com

Fierce Fabulous Genderqueer

To all of the trans queers out there who walk in the world
as you are wearing fabulous clothing and makeup-or
none at all,
to all the buzz cuts and bathroom warriors, I thank you.
To those of you who do go through the hard work to
become you I applaud you.
To those who have lost families and made your own know
that I stand as one of you.

To those who wear the scars on the inside not the outside
who cannot reveal the truth of self,
I honor you. I stand to give you strength to find the voice
needed to say this is who I am.

I did not shave my head until my mother was dead.
I did not embrace the term queer, really, until I was 50.
Only my close friends call me **HE** because
even though others see me as he they still use the
"correct" pronoun she.
I've finally stood up and said, this is who I am.
Declared it publicly I am here and genderqueer.
And while I've tried the label trans, it still doesn't suit my
fluidity
Gender is too elusive to hit the T.
(this has since changed)

All of my life I've been on the outside. Boxes and labels fit
like oddly shaped clothing.
Lesbian, fag, gay, these terms did not quite seem
appropriate.
So today I take back that word I used long ago
QUEER
and I say to you now this is who I am.
Not quite male not quite female, two-spirit,

Embodied in Levi's and t'shirts.

Today I say to the world
I am genderqueer.
And I am fierce
I have a place in this world.
So. Do. You.

Words Matter

Words have power
They matter
In conversation
Words can convince
Make you believe
Even if you are lying
Words have power
just ask a preacher
The Pusher
The advertiser
the POTUS
Thoughts create words
Creates form,
Creates reality
Binds us together
Ask the novelist
the songwriter
The poet
Words make us laugh
Cry,
Sigh
Words have power
Words matter.
Speak carefully
To create the reality
You want
Speak the patterns
Of change.

Trans-Body

Take this body
Born
Female
Brain
Not so much
Learns from brothers
Ideas of
male-
Female

This mind can project
A series of stories
All strung together
All ready to be captured
In
One
Single
Moment.

This
Moment in time
I wrap my mind around
Keep brain busy
Stays calm
Ready for a change

Christina Hauck

Christina Hauck was born in Berkeley, CA and grew up near there. She moved to Manhattan, Kansas in 1994 where she taught literature at Kansas State University. She currently lives in Lawrence, KS. Her poems have appeared in many small journals, most recently *Monterey Review*, *Stone Circle Review*, and *Collateral*. She has poems forthcoming in *Coal City Review*, *Flint Hills Review*, and *Streetlight Magazine*.

Alive

It was in Mexico I understood the universe
doesn't care. I missed the safe channel
waded across Garrafón in fins. Ocean caught
and knocked me to my knees
dragged me back and forth along the coral.

When I finally fell clear of the reef
water filled my face mask and snorkel.
I ripped them off to breath and scissored my legs
In water alive alive in air.

~

This poem Originally appeared in Monterey Review.

Christina Hauck

Under the Wing of an Angel

She's been told there is no absolute silence
that if you listen closely you will hear a bird call
or wind turn a leaf or blood course upward past your ear.

Wanting to believe, she returns to the edge of the forest
where trees give way to hard dirt, cyclone fence
a field beyond. She closes her eyes listening
with both ears and every hair on her head.
No sound, not the merest
scrape of a beetle.

She opens her eyes and sees, far off,
across the vast field—
or imagines she sees—a smudge that is smoke
or the dust a tractor raises or a motorcycle
or boys kicking a ball.

And because there is movement there must be sound
or so she reasons, listening there at the edge of the woods
where dogwood flowers and tiny violets and silence

silence that fills her, seeps through pores,
enters her mouth, lungs, brain, till she hangs
like a bell, half in shadow, half in sun; paralyzed; mute.

~

This poem originally appeared in Bakunin.

Christina Hauck

Easter

for my mother

Her skin, thin as rice paper
tears easily. She shows me
where the nurse forgot to peel
the tape that held the IV in place.
At home, when she lifted it off
the seven layers of skin adhered.
She bled for hours. She didn't know
who to call. It seemed the muscle showed.
Now this scab, dark as dried beef.

I tear lettuce into bite-sized squares.
She shows me her wrist
the blue-black dislocation she worries
is a fracture. It's the drugs she says
there's nothing I can do, my bones
are brittle. Breadsticks
I think, moving from counter to stove
from wedges of tomatoes to the thick red
sauce I stir. I salt boiling water
drop tangles of pale green linguini
toss salad with my fingers, burn
my tongue on the spoon.
                                    After we eat
we play scrabble. While she thinks, I drift
from the small round table, the two women
the bright light. Once, I nursed at her breast.
When you were a baby she tells me shyly
you'd sit on my lap for hours while I read
and never whimper or cry. Sometimes
I forgot I held you. I spell

doubt and *do* and count the value

seventeen, eighteen. Let's eat dessert
she cries, remembering the candy tucked
in the white paper sack. I bring out two
truffles, egg-shaped, one pink, one green
and cut them in half. We share them fairly
strawberry and creme de menthe.

At parting we hold each close enough
to almost heal the gap—like Christ
wounded, alive.

~

This poem originally appeared in Bakunin.

Carlos Velez

A writer, musician, poet, composer, and producer, Carlos Velez lives in his hometown of Topeka, Kansas with his partner Elaine and her three kids.

As the music artist Scurvy Rickets, he creates music of all kinds including instrumental piano and chamber music, folk and rock songs, hip-hop and anything else that strikes his fancy.

As the founder of Top City Records, he is actively engaged in the local arts community of Topeka, Kansas, supporting poetry and author groups and producing music with local songwriters and musicians.

A hobbit by nature, he loves a quiet life of hot coffee, moody music, the best of friends, cozy books, and good love.

This Old New Life

In this old, new life
I am well behaved
and misbehaved at times
In moderation
and sometimes with intention

In this old, new life
I have roots that spread
Networks in the soil
My fingers are threads of light
reaching into weavings
of shimmering energies

In this old, new life
I have fun
I laugh and I joke
I dance
Unafraid
Setting the mood, and the stage

In this old, new life
I observe and I focus
I spin the forces of creation in others
With breath and with attention
In this old, new life

The Fool

He washes up on shore.
The fool.
Wrecked and ravaged by the storm.
He set out with naive knowledge and foolish confidence.
Unceremoniously he is dumped on the sand,
rejected by the sea.

The world, like his past, is a spinning blur.
He knows there was life and love in the rolling hills of
memory,
as he knows there are street lights blazing
in the streets of the town just past the moonlit hills
behind him.
He stands, still facing the sea,
unsteady, unfocused.

Courage he does not lack,
but doubt holds him fast.
He had been so sure,
and he cannot see that he was wrong.
He was not wrong.
It was simple chaos that mastered his vessel
and broke the safety of his craft and skill.

His vision slowly clears, but he cannot tell.
His eyes turn liquid.
His grief runs rivers through him
and salts the sea
with each incoming tide rushing around his feet.

The Death Card

Isn't it a kind of death?
An ending of one's self in the world.
A line at its terminus.
A code broken.
Isn't it against the very nature of life to choose a death?
He cannot shake the feeling.

Yet, also, he knows there is no room in this life rebirthed.
Time is short. Life is full.
He has limits, and he has desires.
A great love it would be, the greatest.
He feels the pull of it.
A legacy to leave of himself in the world,
as the years go by and his time grows ever shorter.
What peace to have made your greatest creation.
What joy to see it wrapped in life of its own.

Alas, his legacy will not be so easily won.
His creations only beginning to take form.
What life they give,
work still to be started, nurtured, grown, fulfilled.

He sits at his double-stacked piano,
scraps of music littered about, stories untold, works
undone,
and plays a solitary note.
Again.
Again.
The note rumbles a dirge in solemn procession.

Joan Koromantee

Joan Koromantee was born in Ft. Campbell, Kentucky but has lived in Kansas for many years. She received her Bachelor of Art in Sociology/Psychology from Washburn University in 1983 and completed her Master of Social Welfare from the University of Kansas in 2007. She has spent her career working in various Mental Health facilities. As an artist, she is multifaceted including visual art, Jazz percussion, as well as a poet. Using the medium of art and the process of art making, her work reflects her interest in social justice and the importance of artistic expression as a means of augmenting mental wellness. Her visual artwork has been exhibited in solo exhibitions in Topeka, KS, and on both coasts and she has performed poetically with Jazz artists throughout the Midwest, New York, and Los Angeles. Joan is the author of three poetry books and has been published in several literary magazines. After an extended hiatus, Joan is currently compiling a fourth poetry manuscript.

Yes...I meant PISSED OFF

I choose my words
carefully
Cause sometimes my acid tongue
must become as soft as cotton
while my thoughts
are razor-sharp steel

I choose my words
skillfully
Cause sometimes my eyes
appear warm and inviting as candlelight
Tho my x-ray vision
can clearly discern the bones
of your lies through the flesh
of your deceit

I choose my words
artfully
Cause sometimes my ears
must cease listening as I shrink my overstanding
just to inflate your absurdity
sticky vestiges of your notions
of superiority and guile

I choose my words
surgically
Cause sometimes my piercing fingers
are tempted to eviscerate
so your intestines spill onto the floor
of your ignorance

Yes
I choose my words
wisely

Cause sometimes my caustic tongue
my piercing eyes
my exhausted ears
and my impatient fingers pulsing with rage
must shapeshift

Just to get your attention

What Some Old People Never Tell...

No
These particular ones are unique
brazenly quiet when they enter your room
walk on tip-toe behind you
gently tap on your left shoulder while standing
on your right side

These particular ones always say the same thing
sometimes in different flavors or colors or songs
but always offer a warning about relying on cell phones
websites, anonymous emails, and toothy grins

These particular ones know to remind you that a shit load
of information
is not always true nor accurate nor useful
and a truck load of knowledge has to ripen
like plump tomatoes on a drooping vine
before it can be called wisdom

Cause wisdom comes with the sheen of experience
bruises, scars, chipped teacups, and backaches
Wisdom comes with getting knocked down to your knees
then struggling upright again
clawing again towards life
Rinse and repeat
and repeat and repeat

These particular ones are deliberate
with stiff worn straw hats pulled low
hinting at museums in faded eyes
authentically gray-haired and bearded
They always challenge with a garden of clever answers
and blue flash drives tucked wisely in back pockets

Antidote to boredom

Today
I'm gonna sip Rum Cokes
savor a bowl of Acapulco-Gold
Re-watch "The Shining" and make-believe
that I am Jack Nicholson
running madly through a snow encrusted maze tightly
gripping
a raised axe
frantically hunting relentless fools
who refuse to let me
enjoy Brussel Sprouts and real butter, butter
in peace
celebrate this flame-tinted sunset
Then
I'll take a nap

Jaedon Blocker

Jaedon Blocker, also known as Arranging the Pieces, is a 21-year-old poet from Topeka, Kansas. He has been writing poetry since he was 17, and his first book *Maybe Someday, Maybe Someday* was released on April 10, 2024, his second book *I Love Him At Last* is set to come out on March 5, 2025, and he is now working on book three. Currently, he is studying Elementary Education at Washburn University and besides writing poetry and teaching, he enjoys playing soccer, obsessing over music, and hanging out at home with his family and cats. He writes to help him arrange the broken pieces of himself, and he hopes that as you read it you will find pieces of yourself within his words and be able to arrange some of your own brokenness.

^ • < —

"We're all broken, and we're just arranging the pieces"

Instagram: @arranging_the_pieces

i'll cut my hair

I sometimes wonder
What it might be like to come back to life
Like a thousand fish forming
A black and white striped kaleidoscope
As the sun rises on an island's coast
Or like ice and snow
Crawling, consuming, controlling deep inside my bones
Would colors effervesce?
And all the mess be called success?
Twenty years I've been depressed
But now I choose how I'll spend the rest

So I ask myself
How I would describe things
If I walked you through my life
Like literally walked you through it
Went back in time
A tour guide of a past life
Look to your left, you'll see a sad sight
A sad kid in a sad life
Making bad choices on bad nights
And up ahead is the very last time
That I felt I'd have something better than a trash life
Though I'm probably not a day past nine
You'd ask "Is that really true?" and I'd say "That's right"
"And I've hated me since that night"
Or would I walk you through with a smile on my face?
Hold myself in a tight and warm embrace
Tell you this is a kid who has lived his life with grace
He's run for miles but still has miles left to race
And he's filled with traumas that consume his frail
headspace
But he's found a voice and words to keep these thoughts
contained

And though no one understands, they will help him bear the pain
So as we walk on forward, Jaedon, I will leave you in this place
Me and my friend here have to get back home, but I can't wait to see how you will change

If I'm being honest
I think I like the second better
It still expresses the struggle
But offers hope that could last forever
I try not to think back too much
I don't want to relive all the pain
But the pain is love and the love is pain
So I guess in the end it's all the same

And who says you can't be reborn!?
Who says you can't go back in time!?
Who says you can't do it over again!?
And change the outcome, where you end up
Without losing the past!?
Who says *I* can't be reborn!?
Who says *I* can't go back in time!?
Well, I'm returning to do it over again!
And change the outcome, where I am now
While embracing my past!
I love him at last

So I'll cut my hair
And I'll wash my face
I know that the past
Cannot be erased
But it can be redefined
It can be rearranged
And we can see there's beauty to find
In the depths of our pain

Since the day I was born
I've been missing pieces of me
And over time I've been broken
Growing increasingly weak
But in words and creation
I've found a reason to breathe
To live for myself and for others
More meaningfully
So if you ever feel like
You're nearing defeat
No one's seeing your feelings
No one's hearing you speak
You'd be better of dead
Your story incomplete
The sky's up above
But you stare at your feet
Just know you don't have to look up
To feel the sun's heat
And through your darkest of times
We will be here, you'll see
And if you can't find a reason to live
Your first reason is me
Because you will always
Be one of the pieces I need
And without you here
I'll always be incomplete

Focus On The Moon

Out in the night
Barely a cloud in the sky
But you can't see the ground
In the endless darkness surrounding you
Just focus on the moon
Focus on the moon
Focus on the moon

The trees blur the boundary between above and below
You can't find your way out, can't find your way home
The sea searches, growing rougher as it flows
It can drown your heart out, as its beat starts to slow
The leaves rustle loudly, breathing all you've ever known
You lose sight of what's ahead, you lose sight of home
But although you feel like you may have lost all of your
hope
Just focus on the moon, it'll lead you home

Just focus on the moon
Focus on the moon
Focus on the moon
Let the stars fill your view
They'll take care of you
You'll be safe soon
Just focus on the moon

The serpent of your sorrow binds you up inside its coils
Its constriction holds you tight
You'll slowly suffocate here, but you know, but you know
An infection from its bite
As you walk on through the forest, every step becomes a
struggle
No protection from the plight

Let yourself be illuminated by the moon's glow, by the
moon's glow
A reflection of the light

Take the bit of light you have and find your way
Fix your eyes, try to focus, clear your head of the pain
And as the mud piles on your clothes, colors covered by
cracked clay
No matter what, — don't be deceived, it's not a stain

Just focus on the moon
Focus on the moon
Focus on the moon
Let the stars fill your view
They'll take care of you
You'll be safe soon
Just focus on the moon

Pull it in a little closer
And let it lift up the tide
So the water can wash away your pain

Just focus on the moon
Focus on the moon
Focus on the moon
With all that life has put you through
Looking on the bright side's not an easy thing to do
So just hold on, hold the hope you have
The sun will come out soon

Just focus on the moon
Focus on the moon
Focus on the moon
Focus on the moon

Running with Hope

4 a.m.
I put on my shoes and head outside
Hoping my path will lead me to hope
You see...
Hope is a runner
And I feel like I'm always running after him
But never feel that I can catch him
Hope runs marathons just for the thrill
I run out of breath at every hill
I wish I had that kind of strength
  but don't think I ever will
Then he comes up behind me
Takes my hand, helps me run
And we run together toward the sunrise
But, by the time it has risen
Hope is way up ahead, out of reach
...yet again
Still, I keep chasing all morning
But as the sun rises higher
My pace just fall lower
Until hope is far out of sight
  and I'm left in his dust
By noon, I'm laying face-down in the dirt
Trying to claw forward
And escape the claws of the oncoming nightfall
But, fingers blistered, clothes stained
Shoes tattered, sun-baked
I turn my head,
   see the footprints of the steps I've taken
   and the stars coming into view
   as I get passed by the afternoon;
   I just let time slip on by
And, on my knees, I retrace my steps

(Though, looking back on it later, I realize this was a sign
to keep moving forward, running toward the sun, backlit
by the stars—the battles I've won)
Then I get up,
    the darkness and I bounding toward one another
    like long-lost lovers
But I keep tripping on my laces—my thoughts
    the ones I've let loose until they trip me up and tie me
down
And there I am...again
Face-down in the dirt, making mud with my tears
And I keep sinking down, coated deep in my fears
Pit-pat, pit-pat
(The sound of hope gliding lightly, barefoot across the
landscape)
Heart now beating in my chest, I glance up and see
His glimmering eyes,
    begging me to keep breathing, keep seeking
He ties up my laces
    and wipes the mud off my face then
    smiles at me
And tells me to keep chasing

^ • < −

"Hope will never stop running . . . it's up to you to keep
up"

Thomas Kennedy

Tom Kennedy is a retired English professor. He has been trying to write poetry for sixty-six years.

Stone, ancient, quiet, tough, I will become

Stone, ancient, quiet, tough, I will become
as quiet as an ancient stone, no more
tossing about or restless stretching for
the hard to reach, no comment, silent, dumb.
I will become a mineral again
like mountains, deserts, dirt, and be once more
as quiet as a stone, and be once more
a part of what I was since time began,
forever quiet, years of quietness,
no lexicon, no sentence fragments, run-
on sentences, verbosity, unnec-
essary wordiness, and no redun-
ancy, no iambs, anapests, or rhyme,
at home again until the end of time.

Not Everything That Happens

Not everything that happens is a poem:
some lovers love and never write a sonnet,
some soldiers die without an epitaph,
nightingales sing somewhere without an ode,
some hypocrites are never satirized,
and some revenge has no soliloquy.
Not everything that happens is a poem:
stars burn unseen in distant galaxies,
and time will end without a metaphor.

Kay Duganator

Kay Duganator is a Kansan born and raised. Her artistry includes poetry, fiction, and story telling. Kay can be heard reading her work at Speak Easy Poets and other open mic venues around the Midwest.

Kay has been a featured poet/host at The Wheel Barrel Open Mic Night and featured at their event Sounds of Strength. As well as a past feature at a People's Poor Campaign event. Kay got the chance to perform on the legacy stage at the 2018 and 2019 Aaron Douglas Art Fair. Recently she was the April feature for Poetry Munch based out of Lawrence, KS.

She is the current host for the first of its kind event in Topeka, Noto Story Slam. She also had the honor of being the host for the 2018 P.O.E.T Unity Festival held in Chicago, and the Poetry Pavilion at the 2019 Aaron Douglas Art fair.

She has been interviewed on Marcia Epstein's *Talk with Me*, as well as Washburn University's radio show *Sunflower Sutras*, and Two Wolves *Meet the Artist*. Her voice has also been used for a Jefe Fashion commercial.

She has also been nominated for the 9th annual Dubceez Underground Entertainment Awards as the Best Female Spoken Word Artist and nominated for Best Newcomer in the Second Annual Music and More Poetry Awards. Kay, writing as "Kayla Dugan" won honorable mention with her short story entitled *Lions* in the Topeka Zoo's Adult Writing Contest 2019. Kay won the Best Host for the National Spoken Word Awards 2020.

A few of her works can be found in *Quivira, The Best of ESU, The Tin Lunchbox, The Blue Mountain Review, Writing From the Center* and *Ichabods Speak Out*. Kay has also released two chap books. One is entitled *The Beast Within*, which released in 2018 and is a collection of flash fiction. The second *Small Visions* which released in 2019 is a collection of micro poetry.

Kay Dugantor will be releasing a new chapbook this year called *Planting Seeds*.

Food Brought to My Table

Every guest brings food to my table.
So I was only mildly surprised
by your offering of words.

I took your poem, to add to the soup.
Scraping off the letters and mixing
them in slowly with my wooden spoon.

They sink below the surface,
and we make uncomfortable eye contact.
You clear your throat as I say,
The words will help the soup thicken.

I offer you a beer and apologize
for the taste of regret.

This batch is more bitter
I say, popping off the top.
I take one for myself,
closing the fridge door
on casseroles that taste like grief.

New beginnings are made up of pie
and cookies double as a thank you.

the soup bubbles and I decide
it must be done.

I can tell right away the poem
mixed in well with my own hopes and dreams.
A warm kind of soup that soothes the soul.

We both slurp down your words
of the world's beauty,

at least the way you see it.

I pack a container when we are both finished
so you can take some poetry home with you.

We complete the night
with a cup of coffee on the porch.

I had added a pinch of hope to each.
Hope, must be used sparingly,
because it is so sweet.

Read Between the Lines

Always read between the lines.
To fully get every side of the story.
This way you can enjoy extra helpings
of your favorite tale.
Every book is twice as long
when you read it backwards and forward.
Maybe if you read it upside down
you can see the other side.
Every question I've ever had
has been answered when I've examined every side.
I can only read one book each season
it takes time to read this way.
Yet I've never been left unsatisfied
when I read inbetween the lines.

Tara Rhiannon Bartley

Tara Rhiannon Bartley is a mixed media artist, poet, zinester, and local cryptid. They enjoy iced chai and hiding their face in fuzzy tummies.

Their written works have been featured in *Kansas Time + Place*, the *Transvetia* zine, *Tittynope Zine*, *Swedish Apache Press*, some other places, and now here. Howdy (ˆ ౪ ˆ)

Your Last Breath

I'm told I'll always feel you
in my heart.
But in truth,
I feel you most
in my lungs.
I feel you most
in the choking sobs,
in the jagged sniffles,
in the rapid fire succession
around 2AM.

You take my breath
every time I think
of your last.

You Stopped Smiling

The feeling of my heart churning
as it thumps into my pillow
keeps me up long enough
to force my valves into decision.
In -　　　　　*I wonder how true it is for me*
　　　　　　to long to be the dead
　　　　　　child I can see
　　　　　　In all of Mom's pictures.
　　　　　　Age three: "That's when
　　　　　　You stopped smiling."
Out -　　　　*I listened to records instead*
　　　　　　of working again,
　　　　　　with fantasies going to bed.
　　　　　　Images of me as flash cuts
　　　　　　in my head I am a male
　　　　　　singing.
Two pounds of cotton between us,
but still I can feel the pounding,
unrelenting.
It begins to hurt.

Dead Bird Near The Window

You lay under the countless visions
of us student passers-by.
We are busy.
Too busy.
But I've become enveloped in this antithesis of
permeability.
Such a small detail,
why should we bother
to be bothered
by macabre derails
of our comforts, of our schedules, of our responsibilities.

So on you I continue to return a curious gaze.
Unrelenting awareness,
a morbid needing
to watch in-between my classes
As you decay atop Henderson's 2nd floor roof.
You're open;
Opening apart.
Rotting forever more and more,
every day progressing,
Furthering your nothingness about you
as you're poorly hidden by shy leaves of numerous
culminated falls,
all on a building for people just walking through,
obligation still demands completion.

But I, with eyes transfixed,
I'm compelled to stare at you,
Chthonic to accept you,
dead morning dove apotheosis,
honesty bared rawest for us all,
a sky burial beneath the noses of drifters.

Adam White

Adam White tries his best to be a decent enough human being. He is on an ongoing artistic journey. Vultures are his favorite animal.

The Hopeful Scavenger

I'd like to believe I suffer from an acute case
of coulrophobia, but sometimes I think
I'm the real clown. Clinging to family and friends,
telling my therapist the horrors of my existence.
I just like being comforted, can't seem to get enough.

My laugh becomes embedded in the background beat of
life,
lost in the rhythm, scattered among melodic notes.
Love letters, veiled threats, wrathful rants.
The grudges gurgle up from otherwise mundane mud,
suddenly slinging obscenities at phantoms from days
long since

withered away. Shrill and shriveled I try to embrace
the tragedy of a sad clown. Operatic maybe, a figure on a
stage,
constantly saber-rattling at those who rattle my cage.
But if I'm a kind of bird, I'd like to believe I'm a buzzard,
feared by some, looked at in disgust by most.

Sometimes I think someone up there still smiles upon me
though,
laughs like thunder, the joy in their eyes sparkling like
lightning,
watching me feast on carrion, free of judgment and free
of hate.

Exegesis

My demons are coming, and they're bringing cookies.
Perpetually sweetening sins, I bite into a dozen of them,
gorging on hypnosis, robotic transformation, too much
information.

      I still talk to God sometimes . . .

I'd like to take Occam's razor and shave Pascal's wager
a little. Save it as a trinket or dangling
memento.

      The precipice of insanity seems to draw nearer
every painful weekend . . .

The pensive paradigm I find myself in is a real danger,
mental handcuffs to be bound in.

      Dear Almighty Encephalon, please forgive our
trespasses as we forgive
those who have ensnared us . . .

An Honest Mistake by The Bravery is a good song,
wish I could sing it to my soul – and actually believe it.

      A trillion tears have fallen, flooded the Earth with
palpable rancor . . .

They've won yet again as I burrow back
into the sleek, sanitary hell
I have crafted for myself.

Dionne A.L. Carter

Dionne A.L. Carter came to write poetry because of a loss. She found her voice at Speak Easy Poets thanks to Sue Edgerton-Johnston. She writes from the heart, and writes about strong women that kicked open doors for which we are grateful.

Glory Fist (a tribute to Gloria Steinem)

See these hands?
These hands rock babies, scrub floors, work in factories,
the typing pool, the great outdoors.
But my mind wanders free, aching to break the bonds
that hold these hands in their bent, worn position
Kept in my place by a society that doesn't value my
vision.

A vision of woman. A future where we are equal.
Where little girls that want to be doctors are not told to
be nurses,
Where we are paid the same for our verses,
Where the word woman doesn't evoke curses,
Where we are not regulated to 2nd class status even in
our churches.

You felt our pain, you saw us all, you heard the longing
and answered the call-
We answered with our weathered hands breaking the
bonds as they curled into fist,
As we found our voices, letting out a mighty roar-
We would no longer be silenced.
We will not fade into the background
Feel the earth quake as with our fist we pound
And it cracked, then crumbled....

All you Glories...thank you for bearing the weight of the
stones, smashing like waves against the barricades,
Red faced men so absurd, hurling "feminist" as if it was a
dirty word.
Ignoring the word "no", said in countless refrain
The glass ceiling hurts when it shatters
Guess that's why it called window pane.

You absorbed that pain from the teenager that now had a
choice
From the house maid that now had a voice
From the secretary who moved to the corner office
From the little girl who could now say, "welcome to my
doctor's office".

Our fist unfurled, hands held high, fingers splayed as we
rejoice
At the freedoms our mothers didn't have
At the freedoms our daughters will have
Equality is in all our grasp.

You keep leading as we shed our scars
We will keep reaching for the stars.

Striking Sandman:

Sleep eludes me...
The back of my closed eyelids become the canvas for the
projection of our story; cut short.

The soft look in your eyes. The belly shaking laugh out
loud of your joy. The taste of red wine sampled from the
pout of your lips. The heat of your body as you curve into
the crook of my arm, made just to fit you. The weight of
your head on my shoulder as you relax fully in peaceful
repose. The crease of your brow, smoothed away by my
touch as your eyes close.

He visits you, but evades me...
As in the day, harsh reality bleeds through, as only in
dreams can I have you, hold you.

Now I lay me down to sleep, but sleep eludes me. The
Sandman is on strike, withholding what I so desperately
need. Finally, he comes and I can see you, hold you into
the night.

A new day dawns, eyes open and the sweet relief of rest
gives way to utter loneliness.

Maya Fly...

"I've learned that people will forget what you said, people will forget what you did, but people will never forget how you made them feel." - Maya Angelou

People will never forget what you said.
You spoke volumes, shining a light that casts out the dread.
Teacher of many, activist for all, your words heralded, love, peace, freedom, equality, like a trumpet's call.
Lectures and poems slip in smooth cadence from full lips, received by thirsty ears, traveling to starving souls, setting fires of knowledge and inspiration, giving us the keys to our salvation.

People will never forget what you did.
You gave us prose that spoke of the mother land, that spoke of this land, that spoke of our oneness; that inspired us to take a stand.
You caused Women to treasure their hearts, embrace the swell of their hips and love the sway in their walk, phenomenal woman, that was she. Phenomenal women, that is we.
You wrote of struggle, and carried yourself with pride when the words Negro and woman we used to chastise.
Yet you embraced humanity and gave us a buoy on which to cling, when you helped us to discover why the caged bird sings.

People will never forget how you made them feel.
There is power in your words, felt by every generation when you wrote "Bringing the gifts that my ancestors gave, I am the dream and the hope of the slave. I rise" Speaking to that next generation of marchers you proclaimed that "The ancestors remind us, despite the

history of pain, we are a going-on people who will rise
again."
Words of wisdom and a life of humbleness leave an
indelible imprint on humanities consciousness.
Never forgotten, in the constriction of our hearts when
you spoke of what binds us together and what tears us
apart.
Never forgotten, the swell of our pride when you told us
in love we have nothing to hide.
Never forgotten, the cleansing deep of our sigh, when
you told us to drop our burdens and learn to fly.

So, fly away bird, soar ever high
As we dry our tears and promise with pride
To follow your path and continue to rise

Yolanda Wilson

Yolanda Wilson has called Topeka her home for over 40 years. She is an active member of the LGBTQ community. She graduated from Washburn University with a creative writing degree in 2006. Her poems *After the March* and *The Midnight Hour* are published in the Inscape 2001 magazine. Yolanda is a proud mother, aunt, and great aunt!

Intimacy

I was congested
Could not breathe
Brother gave a
Benadryl to me
Ten minutes into
Tales of the City
I began to snore
Heard him angry
Wanting to wake me
You defended me
While rubbing my back
Never had I felt
Security like that

Over thirty years past
Somehow the longing fades
Another woman came
Taking a place
Only ever mine
In my dreams
As decades roll by
I still remember
Your touch
Warm and tender

Sometimes at night
I wonder
Will intimacy
Come again
I know now
What I didn't know then
How deeply I could fall
For a woman
And friend

Mountains

Mountains may cry as they crumble
Yet give prayers of praise
As pebbles on the ground
Thankful to the Creator for
Another chance to be useful
Upon their journey of existence

Pebbles spent into sediment
Blown by wild winds onto
Ocean floors will worship with water
Honored to wave to the
Highest heavens as
Sand washed to shore

So too must we rejoice like rocks
In all aspects of our lives
When we are lifted up like mountains
Fallen to the plains like pebbles
Sunken like sand in the sea
In every moment there is blessing

You Don't Have to Kiss Me

you don't have to kiss me
just hold me one more time
run your hands over my skin
like you did when you were mine

put your fingers inside me
do that thing that you do
to make me scream
to make me sing
and spread my love
all over you

then let me taste you

your moaning
makes me wet
my hand
between your thighs
watching you
roll back your eyes

until we both
reach that plane
the explosion
of the brain
all senses ignite
and we're on fire
no one could ever
take me higher

bodies flailing
sheets on the floor
both exhausted
wanting more

we make love
long through the night
and twice again at dawn
when you think
there's nothing left
i inspire you to go on

you move me
like no other lover could
setting my skin on fire
putting my soul at ease
please touch me
let me feel that way again

you don't have to kiss me
just hold me one more time
like you did when we were lovers
like you did when you were mine

Emily Fincher

Hi my name is Emily Fincher, I use my writing as an outlet. Fighting anxiety and depression daily is a horrible struggle, but I use writing to help me cope. Though my poems are grim, I refuse to give up.

Running With My Wolves

Now I know why I yearned to cry
Now I know why and I can say I'm fine
Dancing my way through the pain
Learning to dance in the rain
Finally taking flight and soaring through the night
Dancing to the beat of my heart, I promised myself to not fall apart
I found years of misery but now it's disappearing
I'm finding hope, finding that I can cope
It hurts to not know why she'd ever try
It hurts that it's been stuck in my mind for such a long time
It's hurts and it has left a burn
But tonight I'll be at peace with my demons, I'll let them know I'm not leaving, I'm done grieving
And now I'm telling myself to never let go for I now know now I'm getting this wolf off my back and learning to run with the pack

Broken heart, picking up the parts
Putting it together like a puzzle, taking the courage to remove my wolves muzzles
I know how easily they can bite but I will fight
I know how easy it is to let my heart be consumed, but I'm saving room....
Saving room for love and to know that I am enough
It's not my fault that she left, and I'm starting to accept the theft
The theft of my happiness that was taken before my eyes, I'm fine
I know well enough that I am loved
And I refuse to give up by my own hand, I'm learning how to stand
I'm learning what it means to be me

Once more I pick myself up off the floor
I will now enjoy myself, no longer living life like I'm in
hell
Accepting the facts she's never coming back
And that's okay I know I'll stay
And now I'm getting this wolf off my back and learning to
run with the pack

I'm learning to be fixed, emotions are mixed
But I don't care, I'm finding how to find it fair
I'm leaning into the reality, it's not my fatality
I'll be free, I'll be me!
It was never my fault so I'm letting the guilt leave, and I'll
stop the grief
Feeling empowered, no longer a fragile flower
Capable of banishing my demons, they'll be fleeing
I'm learning that this road may be lost but I will pay the
cost
To live life, with no strife
I will learn to walk on the fading lines, I'll learn in time
I'll find my heart among others like me, but I'll set us free
Doves in a cage, for so long it's been surrounded with
rage
But opening that cage with the key, now watching them
finally be free
And now I'm taking this wolf off my back and learning to
run with the pack

I'm learning how to run, I'm learning how to love
Fallen on the cement, needed to vent
Sending everyone who left in that way my prayers
I cried for you long enough, now I'll pick myself up

.....

Taking a break from running with my wolves, facing my
goals

Face to face with the very thing that kept me down, but now Im free from the silent sound
She's raging and her teeth are sharp, but yet I find this hard.....
Reaching my hand to pet her head, to let her know I'm not letting go
I'm in charge and she is not, I can control these thoughts
She let me pet her head and no longer am I feeling dead
I was able to tame the emotions, barely any commotion
I was able to set myself free, and come back to reality
Accepting the facts, she's never coming back
But that won't keep me from living, I'll be giving.......it my all
Now I run with my pack and I got her off my back
I run with my pack and I got her off my back
I run with my pack, accepting the facts
And yet it's a journey and not immediately will I be healed I will learn what it means to feel
I got her off my back..and now I run with the pack

Throwing Myself Off The Edge

The curtains fall, and soon I hear a familiar voice call
I follow the voice, and am met with a choice
Down the light wood I can go, or I can venture into the
unknown
I walk down a strange place, looks like the trees all have a
face
I met a riverbed, but something wasn't right, it was red in
the night
I followed the red water to a cliff, soon there was a
sudden shift
A shift in the energy around me, soon it got hazy
I walked to the edge of the cliff, and soon heard
something click
I turned around to see me, myself, I?
But it doesn't make sense, she died
The girl I used to be, no that can't possibly be she
I haven't seen her in years, this has to be my fears
Disguised as my yearning in life
I walked up by she, this couldn't possibly be
I reach out my hand, she reaches out hers, we align, and I
see the signs
Signs that she is who I used to be, she is me

I moved my hand in a peculiar way, she obeys
I soon asked, "What are you doing here? You're part of my
past, here you aren't supposed to be, do you need to tell
something to me?"
She took a step towards me, and asked "Why are you
leaving me for dead?"
I looked at her in an odd fashion, I could feel the tension
"What are you talking about?"
I was so confused, and conflicted, and she could sense it
I then watched as she held her hand out to mine, she then
said, it was time

I looked around, and still saw the red river flowing next to me
I asked her what it was, she simply replied, "Your sinful blood. Don't you remember what you did to us, to our arms, to our body, to our mind??"
It came back to me with time
I remembered what I did, but the sadness I couldn't bid
I tried to comply, but she screamed at me, "WHY DID YOU LEAVE ME TO DIE???"

"I'm trying I swear, I promise I did care!!"
She cried, "YOU LEFT ME TO WILT, YOU LEFT ME TO THE GUILT, DO YOU KNOW HOW FAST I DECAYED, DO YOU KNOW WHAT IT FELT LIKE TO KNOW YOU DIDN'T STAY?????"
I screamed at her with tears flooding my eyes, telling her I tried
She then pulled out a knife, she plans to take my life
Replacing me with her, I'll be that past girl
She ran at me at full speed, cutting my arms, I fall to my knees
I tried so hard to forget what I did to myself, I tried to crawl my way out of that hell
I tried with all my might, to not be consumed by the night
But alas past me is haunting me constantly
I can't help but remember what I did do her body, I can't help but start sobbing
I can't help but think about the pain I caused, I can't help but cry because she lost
She then got over me, and I struggled to get her off, I can't be her, she's too lost
I managed to push her off, while trying to get her to stop

I grabbed the knife that fell on the ground, and told her to stop this violent round

She screamed my name, and said "I WENT FUCKING
INSANE!!!"
I screamed at her to stop, but instead she ran at me with
full speed and pushed me off the edge, then screaming
"YOU FUCKING PLEDGED"
Holding onto a tree branch that was protruding out of the
side of the cliff, but it broke so swift
I fell, and fell down to the blood Red Sea beneath me
I fell into my sinful blood, and drowned in my forbidden
love
The love I had obtained after the first cut, to do so felt
like a must
I screamed her name, I screamed from the internal pain
I cried for her to forgive, for once upon a time we did live
I cried to her to set herself free, please be happy
"Remember the dreams you dreamt, hold them close,
hold them tight, for soon you'll lose sight"
I screamed her name one last time, and said "DON'T LOSE
TO TIME!"
As I feel myself sink farther into my sinful blood, I feel it
all again, cuts start to align my skin
I go numb, and fall into a certain type of love
I am in love with the pain, I am in love with my sinful rain
I fall once more, and die at my core……..

My Broken Masquerade

Crystal chandeliers were hanging from the ceiling, but the paint on the walls was peeling
The room glistened with jewels and lights, but I could tell it was another disguised fight
I could tell, this wouldn't go well
Everyone was wearing masks, and some asked.....
Some asked me if I was afraid, I didn't want to say
Soon music started to play, and everyone was dancing gayly
I was approached by a man in a mask, to dance he would ask
I couldn't say no, so I let him and I go
He took my hand, and in the middle we were to stand
But as we started to dance, I fell into a trance
My mind was distracted, and it was weird how I acted
But deep inside, I knew tonight, I was going to die

He grabbed my waist, and told me I'm a waste of space
I finally fell out of the trance, and stopped the dance
I looked around to see all my enemies
As I watch them take off their masks, I met with my past
I looked at who was my dance partner, and almost screamed, this has to be a dream!
My worst foe, to whom I can't let go
I start to run at full speed, I can't be their feed
I won't let myself be devoured, I won't give them that power
The halls became endless, and I was left defenseless
The walls began to cave in one me, it's obvious I'll never be free
Coming to a dead end, I realize myself I can't defend
I begin to back away, but end up in the arms of harm

I'm taken back to the ballroom where it is now dark, and
cold, and I watch as my life unfolds
Their masks are all gone, and I'm starring at everything
that is wrong
Fear, despair, woe, dolor, anguish, guilt, distress, and
regret, how I do fret
One moment they were all wearing colorful clothes of
gold and rose, but now a threat they pose
My broken masquerade has come into play, and I'm not
okay
I feel as the room starts to rotate, and the exit I try to
locate
But the doors disappear, and I'm left with my worst fears
Trying to hold on, everything stops, and is still, but that
doesn't mean good will
The room is now silent and my foes grow violent
In the middle, as I'm made to solve their riddles
Screaming their chants in my ears, I begin to fall with my
tears

I fall to my knees, and pray to God, to vanquish these
horrible odds
I grab myself, and curl into a ball, slowly I feel myself fall
Slowly I fall through the floor, till I can see no more
I fall through the curtains of time, and space, but no
longer am I face to face....with my foes
I prayed to God to help me get out, and to escape my
doubts
But I see now, I've got to do this somehow
I then screamed, "I KNOW YOUR NAMES, YOU WILL BE
TAMED"
Slowly, but surely I feel myself ascend from the void, now
I've got a choice....to make
I can stay or I can go, but only one will lead me home
I shut my eyes tight, and think of the light

When I open my eyes, I'm back in the ballroom, with my
despair, and gloom
I start to feel them all cave in on me, I'll never be free it
seems
I thought I could set myself free, but now I see

My mind won't allow my that opportunity, now I'm part
of the broken community
The community of others who can't escape their demons,
they're seething
They won't leave me alone, I want to go home
The reality of fright, is what I'm going to have to fight
tonight
The reality of shame, these feelings I can't tame
When I fall at the end of the line, then I can truly say I'm
fine
When I'm free from my mentality, when I'm free from the
brutality
When I'm free, when I'm once more me
I think it's safe to say, that I'm forever trapped in my
broken masquerade

James Harrel

James Harrel is a poet, artist, and musician based in Topeka, Kansas, with over 40 years experience writing poetry and drawing. James studied English Literature at Oklahoma City University and the University of Central Oklahoma, and was mentored in poetry writing by MJ McLendon, PhD at the University of Kansas in the late 1990's/early 2000's. James writes about life, love, loss, family, friends, and frequently uses the form of the Sonnet. James also enjoys flower gardening and choral music and has performed with Canterbury Choral Society in Oklahoma City, the Kansas City Symphony Chorus, the Kansas City Fine Arts Chorale, the Topeka Festival Singers, and Shawnee Choral Society.

A Year

A year has passed, and pined away with not
A single couplet rhymed, nor polished phrase
Refined, just countless crude beginnings caught
And crumpled, mired, entombed in the malaise,
This hazy maze of featureless boredom
And uninvited loathsome solitude
Completely drenched in sorrow, soaked in calm
Complacency I slipped away, subdued
The portent of his cruel pronouncement sore
And droning through my head as though it were
Only yesterday that he said "No more"
And with those words the light of day interred.
A year to break the spell of his decree.
A year in search of words to set me free.

Fallen Gemini

We watched the fiery fall of Gemini
Each collapsing in upon herself.
In unison we heard the global cry
Of horror, shock and utter disbelief
Unable to conceive such manifold
Inhuman hatred that conspired to see
These lovely sisters, beacons of the world
Destroyed by such malicious, murd'rous deed.
Is this the end of life as it has been?
Eternal darkness loom, or might there spring
As from the fire-blackened forest, green
New hope for peace, and hatred's healing bring?
We pray, oh fallen sisters, you might shine
And prove the one light by which love we find.

Widow

Two years ago, the cancer took your life
from me. And with it, stole our dreams
of growing old together, like a knife
with surgical precision, left in ruins
the whole of fifteen years I spent with love
reflected back at me when those brown eyes
of yours came into view. We lived above
the darkness, filled our days preoccupied
with all the merry mundane mix and mess
of jobs, our home, the dogs, the garden, cars...
And nights, collapsing side by side to rest
with sweet repose in one another's arms.
We shared our lives a decade and a half
and for that gift, I leave this epitaph.

Duane Johnson

Duane Johnson is a retired journalist, who now primarily writes poetry. He has published two volumes of poetry, *Evolution's Promise*, and *Evolution's Progress*, and is working on another volume of poetry as well as a children's book in collaboration with a well known Topeka artist. He also has published a novel, *Herald of the Resurrection*. He lives in Topeka, Kan., and is married to a retired social worker. They have two grown children. He lives in a modest house with gray siding on a dead-end street, with a chainsaw, fishing gear and kayak in the garage. The near-by four hundred-acre lake is his laboratory.

Timbered Choir

Today his timbered choir sings, bird songs
weaving his words with silence, in rhythm
with leaves. It's Sabbath of course; no church bells
invade this river-edged wood. In red soil
of his Bluegrass farm, his tiller is still
today. Barn doors are closed, and he's strolling
in quiet relief from six days of toil.

This holy day will bow to Labor Day,
an extra respite paid to those who sweat.
I wonder what he'll do to honor time;
meanwhile, he has pad and pen to serve him
until the sun goes down. What to record?
What metaphors and rhymes might incubate?
What lyric will his timbered choir sing?

Immersed in sacred service through his verse,
he keys his voice above the timber's crowns
in harmony with spirits of the soil
then channels earth and heaven with his themes.
Disciples in his woodland chuppah's shade
vow to wed their future to creation
while living light streams through the canopy.

Duane Johnson

The Woman Beneath the Tree

She whispers tales of water signs, moonstains,
and winds of time. She's never known for sure
where she came from; first one family, then
two more. Where she is now seems unsettled.

But she knows her heart's desire, and facing
evening's star, she stands beneath that tree,
her back to it, touching without leaning
against it, considering tomorrow.

The tree, a chestnut oak, firmly rooted,
has traveled eighty times around its star,
drawing rings around its unswerving heart
that throbs to a timeless pulse, still rhythms

invoking winds of time and water signs.
Its growing vantage grants it a grand view
of the lake
            and the woman and the tree
share their blooming visions with each other.

Weathered Together

My hat and I have grown together
weathered together long enough
we can find each other in a crowd.

We came upon each other just this past spring
at a Brian Wilson concert.
That's a story you and I can learn from
about Al and Brian, life-long partners in song
a friendship that outlasted blood
still onstage, that night, fifty years after first performing.

For a while blown apart by a storm
now weathered back together by harmony
voices blending and rising above the applause
finding each other in the crowd.

But I was talking about my hat, I think
and good vibrations we feel when we caress
that redefine us both.
Is that the touch of friendship?
Are we remolded from what we were into whom we are
shaped in part by whom we press close
when in the crush of the crowd?

A week after "Pet Sounds," my hat and I embraced
two honeymooners at a truck stop
their New Orleans home stolen by a storm, then blown to
Kansas.
Weathered together further by four younger, fellow exiles
friendships formed from blood.

To what extent can pilgrims grasp the path beneath their
feet?
Or trees sense soil embracing their roots?

My hat has shared travails with me
secrets you will never know
and oh, the secrets you could share with us, but never
will
for love of friends you have found in the crowd.

Christina Lewis

Christina Lewis loves creating poetry that leaves vivid images in the head and long-lasting effects on the heart. Born and raised in Topeka, KS, she attended Washburn University where she studied Elementary Education. She teaches 5th Grade at Pauline South Intermediate. When she is not writing, she is painting, hiking, enjoying her loved ones, or thrifting.

The Cave

This is a ballad of a bear princess
who stitched her dreams
secretly into seams of her heart
As not to fall prey
to a bloodline contented with
one thousand what always has beens versus
that one CAN BE

To share DNA can expose
your wounds,
your cuts,
your shovels,
your spears
Put them all together haphazardly
and you have generational fear, sing a long
and let these weary strands be set free here

I was protecting
A fierce protector with her swords and fears
for young cubs in her care while
she was all but old
Her bravery, her boldness made her
question her mold
the cold matriarch of the cave albeit caged idly danced
to the quakes and rhythms of the elements once
more

The cave is freezing
Instantaneously icicles fell impaling parts of self
once loved dearly

A series of fixed icy trances,
one solid withdrawn door
Gave chance for play before inevitable perpetual rage
And she'd welcome us back in
right before a thaw of a freeze and
The acid would be poured so generously
between the bars of the caged and as they melted,
the inhabitants were afraid to say,
"I want to be out and not one with you
in your sordid cage"
Oh, I pray for a freeze and undoing to all sadistic thrills.
The cave is burning
Fire pursued,
sometimes consuming
before small feet could board
their dissociative planes

Catastrophically weathered graves
fashioned as toys and books and games
A small girl is singing
with a voice so freeing as clipped wings sear by,
yet another is writing of a life
not so tethered to the weather of another
How would one snuff out an ember
for one acclimated to arson endeavors?
Oh, the fullness to burn and began again

The cave is drowning
But, what would the town say?
We were you... you were us
You are not God, you are dust
An insurmountable pain,
The sting of the violation

The word curses attached to spittle that graced my face
Their letters and syllables churned out formations so
ghastly that new ears would smolder;
new lungs would combust if they did not master
the art of holding one's' breath while being held longer
and longer underwater
I pray for the resurrection of the deep..

The cave is landing!
Passengers of each plane would reengage
to find a spot to land
Security was a surety
since the elements coursed steady in a public place
A trip to the store,
a treasured barbeque eatery,
the library,
a tent cent candy
and the park, the zoo,
the giggles and sweet serenity
of sleep after making shadow animals in the dark

This ends the ballad of a bear princess
who broke out of a congealed cage
The burns meant for her spirit were used to singe holes
in societal ceilings
Feel the healing as souls give up all the stories the
originations of wounds
& cuts
& buried aches
& preservations
For they are blurring the visions
of our sons and daughters

To dream is her proclamation
See there, as she wrenches frozen dreams
By ripping them out of seams

with bloodied teeth for
she did NOT fall prey to a bloodline
drowning beneath one thousand that have tried to
Bequeath their secrets; slinking and slimy like decay
It's sacred rot needing to be severed for
This birthing.. this unearthing
Is not an option, and
We *will* heal on stage
Then between the sets, our Father will reset
and abet a healing
So profound,
We will release,
We will bellow a mighty generational sound
That cancels out all fear
Oh no, it is not welcomed here

This sweet ballad I sing I hold dear, it pools in my chest
As you open the door to my cage, my soul finds rest
I am really here outside of a cage within that cave
At last..... the freezing, burning, and drowning of
maternal rage

The Train

Your whiskers scratched my face
as I snuggled deep into your lap
You reminded me of a black Santa;
your stomach rounded and tightly stretched
Across what I imagined was an overly inflated beach ball,
It made the perfect pillow.
Your laughter shook your form,
you were jolly,
and you were giving;
You did give me life
after all.

Your snores echoed throughout the house like a
wheezing train low on fuel, its frightful howls
somehow managed to
help me get back to sleep
As I would imagine a bright, sturdy red train
coughing up gray, billowing smoke
It had made it home

Then it rained
You were never home,
She told us that you were working,
but I knew better, I saw better
Deep
in the lines of her thinking face
She would cry silent, invisible tears as she
gave us warm baths,
the salt from her tears was a weird concoction
With cottony bubble gum suds
and water park sized ripples I
splashed her, she splashed back

Then all was ablaze
I dreamed of fire on one of your working nights
I awoke, the train had not made it in
I was deeply afraid and cried as the stinging silence
rocked me back to sleep

The moon, it was bright on the night
I grew up
I stood on my tip toes
Waiting, waiting and waiting
To see the train come in around the bin
Its chugging gave me peace and security
Mom shooed me to bed in the nick of time
I was on the tracks,
I had stood too long
My feet were raw
I saw the train come in,
but you had brought home hot coals

Heard too much that night
Learned that matrimony wasn't a sealant
Foundation's crumble, hearts do shatter
But, you did breathe life into me
As well as disappointments,
And life lessons, too
But most importantly,
You gave me all the love that you could give, Dad

You fell short in many ways,
but you also raised me up
in just as many
I am sorry that I haven't wrote you in some time,
but I figure that now is as good a time as ever

I still remember everything you done for me
and for that, I thank you
Please just promise that you'll
be there waiting for me, once my train comes in...
I won't be afraid
I'm not afraid

~

RIP Dad 05/03/2013

Sue Edgerton-Johnston

Sue Edgerton-Johnston grew up near Topeka, Ks. Back in 2013 she was sitting at an LGBTQ bar called Skivvies Bar and Grill located on S Kansas Avenue on a Tuesday night wondering how many poets could be drawn out of the walls if someone went to the DJ stand and grabbed the microphone to use for open mic poetry. After talking to the owner, she contacted the most amazing local poet that she almost sort of knew, named Annette Billings and the two of them cooked up a plan to host a monthly open mic called Speak Easy Poets. It seems to have worked out well. Sue has co-hosted and mc'd the event every month since then.

Sue is married to Lisa Edgerton-Johnston, who she met at the first reading. She has one daughter named Phoebe. Sue works as a para educator in Topeka. Sometimes, she writes poetry.

Para

Backpacks like parachutes

Softening school day landings of little feet into circle
time safety, smiles... firmly, yet gently coaxed patterns of
centers and potty breaks and songs

Then landing

Small untied, retied, retied.....repeating... untied shoes
Home again to unknown nights and haunted mornings

Parachutes...

Transporting dry erased folders laminated in hopes
The chords of communication between half absent
parents and weekday storytellers imagining stories
untold by bruises, sudden inexplicable tears, and silences
falling flat

Parachutes...

Holding... finger painted masterpieces and gold stars and
prize box toys like rip cords fraying against missed
conferences and unattended PTOs

These are small caregiver agonies

Yes... children do fall down
Even on our careful playgrounds... even out of our careful
arms. We see it in the recesses of 7 hours daily, 5 days a
week, 9 months a year... minus snowdays...

Still

I am prepared... pre para... and para pre an enormous
impossibly possible call

I am parachute

Unpacking backpacks

Packing them back up again with conjectured heart
rending fear
Wishing there were no more weekends or evenings or bus
rides to unseeable addresses

Wanting to keep every student in the sure safety of
leggos and love

I am para...

Parachute... packing everything I can of myself into back
packs... for the sky drive home

lightly

lightly,
and with a wacky biorythmic diligent eye of a mad man
carrying a pocket Tao Te Ching or some ancient western
gravel,
lending absurdity to years,
lightly,
someone sneezes
in the still night
a little achoo riding a unicycle down the hall, turning up
in mission cots or a scholar's studies,the sleeping
apartment menagerie is monkeying around with
ownership and three a.m. prophets,
it is lightly,
relieving

fabienne

today... saturn's smallest moon
with the voice of 6 and the eye of a galaxy asks
"mom, what does 'perspective' mean?"

what i don't tell her is that it is a picture... taken in haiti...
of a girl on a shaken island laying hard on the earth
her school skirt singing privilege in a state of no
privilege... pressed.
the loot... framed art, left by some authority in her arms
not worth the heroic effort of returning to rightful
owners who no longer have walls to adorn.
oh, but when she was still running... it was the roof of a
lean to of siblings weathering aftershocks and gravity
under heavier things... or kindling... or currency for a
first, maybe a last meal... or a sip of nonnecrotic water...
or just something... to have.

shot through by the law and left for dead because she is
dead...
foreshadowing a stretched canvas sky housing thousands
of hundreds dying under the rubble of concrete roofs of
card houses just good enough for a dark culture of
nothing.

a quiet warning
for two erected figures to the right of the frame...
leisurely walking like the nuevo rich after the looting...
booty balanced on heads.
and no one else... is there.

i don't tell her that perspective is the picture, laid beside
this one, of 8 foreign cameras held by 8 pairs of hands
there is not one demon among them,
yet, they are compensated for their horrible duty,

and they hover in just the right angle of light,
each at five paces
from a body
from her body
from the girl...

snapping madly for an award winning picture, artfully
cropped for crafty photo journals demanding from
outside humanity, sympathy, outrage, and money, that
will never reach land.
Foreshadowing cavalier smiles and one northwest woman
leaving,
checking the images in the expensive tool of her trade,
her inevitable grieving begging the question of her
proximity at the moment the fourteen year old fell so
loudly and made news ...
foreshadowing the remains of slow progress teetering,
and one man grown hatian standing, centered, in the also
cropped frame,
not looking at the dead, who are too plentiful, but at the
living who's language he has never learned or has just
forgotten...
so likely, himself just orphaned by family extended
through generations and scooped in mounds like the very
earth... if any earth had been left...
into unmarked dump trucks in procession to the wailing
mountains unnamed...
possibly whispering below roars of heavy equipment, "tu
me manques"...
"you are missing from me"...
"i miss you"...
sometimes, i miss breathing.

their names are now known only by god...those who are
accused, convicted, and destroyed only by god in his
fundamental t-vangelical wrath speaking through the

tongues of raving and ranting judges, self ordained in
loathing.
but here... this creole steeple tips catholic voodoo.
the crucifix is a stuffed doll with a crown of pins,
dragging beads and praying in tongues through rum and
fire for a zombie throwing madonna.
here, magic... is magic in any pew.

perspective is the lens bending itself over backward to
refocus time on the invisible history of proud warriors
enslaved by the cost of freedom,
in debt to unyoked colonials and the supermen of greed
who uprooted every stick from the primordial coral,
kicking topsoil to the wind... causing landslides under
the bent thumb of a hemisphere of blindness and
wealth...
repeatedly raped by total power puppets through the
coup of cholera, the coup of starvation, the coup of slow
death in sweatshops that disney shoved down their
throats like food that can no longer be grown, that is
replaced corporately and ransomed in ships leaking oily
business in garbage and shit clogged ports.

perspective is often fleeting... little... and late.

perspective is often a slow and painful mission battling
tumbling walls undying, and then dying also, holding fast
to the hands they swore to feed or free...

perspective is lying violently still... five paces from the
arms that might have held her, now, immortalized body
and whispered to her last young breath like a daughter
"tu me manques"

perspective is the terrible dilemma... of just shooting her
again.

what did i say to my phoebe? saturn's moon moving in so many rings?

"perspective is a point of view... like, where you are standing when you look at something... like a picture."

it is also something... we struggle... to put things into.

"A picture may paint a thousand words,
but a poem paints a thousand pictures".
- Sue Edgerton-Johnson